Guitar Chord Songbook

Ray LaMontagne

ISBN 978-1-4803-9599-2

HAL•LEONARD®
CORPORATION

7777 W. BLUEMOUND RD. P.O. BOX 13819 MILWAUKEE, WI 53213

In Australia Contact:
Hal Leonard Australia Pty. Ltd.
4 Lentara Court
Cheltenham, Victoria, 3192 Australia
Email: ausadmin@halleonard.com.au

Visit Hal Leonard Online at
www.halleonard.com

Guitar Chord Songbook

Contents

Airwaves

Words and Music by
Ray LaMontagne

Where you go - in' Rust - y James? _

(Capo 4th fret)

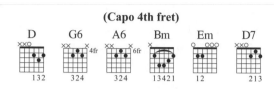

D   G6   A6   Bm   Em   D7

Intro   ‖: D | G6   A6   :‖   *Play 4 times*

Verse 1

D   G6   A6
Where you goin'   Rusty James?

D   G6   A6
To rumble on   knives and chains.

Bm   Em
What you doin'   Betty Sue?

          Bm
She says,   "Whatcha thinkin'?

Em   D G6
I'm comin' with cha.

     A6   D7 G6 A6
I'm comin' with cha."

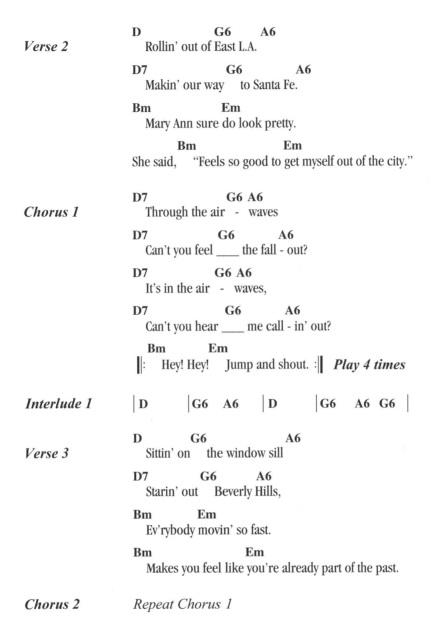

Verse 2

D   G6   A6
Rollin' out of East L.A.

D7   G6   A6
Makin' our way   to Santa Fe.

Bm   Em
Mary Ann sure do look pretty.

         Bm   Em
She said,   "Feels so good to get myself out of the city."

Chorus 1

D7   G6 A6
Through the air - waves

D7   G6   A6
Can't you feel ____ the fall - out?

D7   G6 A6
It's in the air - waves,

D7   G6   A6
Can't you hear ____ me call - in' out?

  Bm   Em
‖:   Hey! Hey!   Jump and shout. :‖ *Play 4 times*

Interlude 1 |D |G6 A6 |D |G6 A6 G6 |

Verse 3

D   G6   A6
Sittin' on   the window sill

D7   G6   A6
Starin' out   Beverly Hills,

Bm   Em
Ev'rybody movin' so fast.

Bm   Em
Makes you feel like you're already part of the past.

Chorus 2   *Repeat Chorus 1*

Interlude 2 |D |G6 |D |G6 |

Verse 4

D   G6   A6
   Where you goin'   Rusty James?

D7   G6   A6
   To rumble on   knives and chains.

Bm   Em
   What you doin' Betty Sue?

        Bm
She says,   "Whatcha thinkin'?

Em   D7 G6
   I'm comin' with cha.

  A6   D7 G6
I'm comin' with cha.

  A6   D7 G6
I'm comin' with cha.

  A6   D7 G6 A6
I'm comin' with cha."

    Bm   Em
Outro   ‖:   Hey! Hey!   Jump and shout. :‖ *Play 7 times*

    Bm Em
‖:   Jump and shout. :‖ ***Repeat and fade***
                         w/ vocal ad lib.

Beg Steal or Borrow

Words and Music by
Ray LaMontagne

So your home - town's _ bring-in' you down. _

Tune down 1/2 step:
(low to high) Eb-Ab-Db-Gb-Bb-Eb

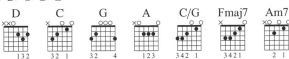

D	C	G	A	C/G	Fmaj7	Am7	
1 3 2	3 2 1	3 2 4	1 2 3	3 4 2 1	3 4 2 1	2 1	

Intro   ‖: D | |C |G   :‖ ***Play 3 times***
                     |D | G |D | G |

                                     D

Verse 1   So your hometown's bringin' you down.

               C   **G**   **D**   **C G**
Are you drownin' in the small ___ talk an' the chatter?

                        D
Are you gonna step into line like your daddy done,

   C   **G**   **D**   **C G**
Punchin' the time and climbin' life's long ___ ladder?

                D
You been howlin' at the moon like a slack-jawed fool

          C   **G**   **D**   **C G**
And   breakin' ev'ry rule ___ they can throw ___ on.

         D
Well, one of these days, it's gonna be right soon,

             C   **G**   **D**   **C G**
You'll   find your legs and go and stay ___ gone.

Chorus 1

A   C/G
Young man, full of big plans

 G   D
An' thinkin' about tomor - row.

A   C/G
Young man, gonna make a stand.

 G   Fmaj7
You beg, steal, you bor - row.

       D
You beg, you steal, ___ you borrow.

C	G	D	
G	D		G

Verse 2

   D
Well, all the friends that you knew in school,

   C   G
They ___ used to be so cool.

       D C G
Now they just bore ___ you.

   D
Well, look at 'em now, already pullin' the plow,

  C   G   D   C G
So ___ quick to take to grain ___ like some old ___ mule.

Chorus 2

A   C/G
Young man, full of big plans

 G   D
An' thinkin' about tomor - row.

A   C/G
Young man, gonna make a stand.

 G   Fmaj7
You beg, steal, you bor - row.

You beg, you steal,

Pedal Steel Solo | D | | C | G | |

You borrow.

‖: D | | C | G | :‖

| D | | G | D | | G | |

Bridge

Am7
Dreamin' of the day you're gonna pack your bags,

            C   D
Put the miles ___ a - way.

            Am7
Oh, just grab your girl and go where no one knows you.

                 C   D   G C D
What will all the old ___ folks ___ say?

Verse 3

                  D
So the hometown's bringin' you down.

     C   G   D   C G
Are you drownin' in the small ___ talk and the chatter?

                  D
Are you gonna step into line like your daddy done,

C   G   D   C G
Punchin' the time and climbin' life's long ___ ladder?

Chorus 3

A   C/G
Young man, full of big plans

     G   D
An' thinkin' about tomor - row.

A   C/G
Young man, gonna make a stand.

     G   Fmaj7
You beg, steal, you bor - row.

                      D   C G
You beg, you steal, ___ you borrow.

Outro | D | | G | D | |

| | G | D | | G | D | ‖

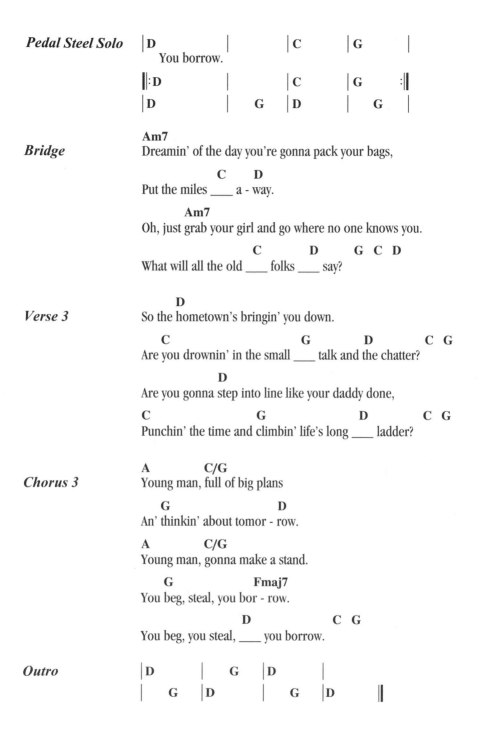

Be Here Now

Words and Music by
Ray LaMontagne

Don't let your mind __ get wea - ry

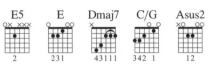

E5   E   Dmaj7   C/G   Asus2

Intro

E5				
E				
Dmaj7				
E				
Dmaj7		C/G		
		E5		

Verse 1

    E
Don't let your mind get weary and confuse your will.

           Dmaj7
Be still, don't ____ try.

    E
Don't let your heart get heavy, child.

                Dmaj7 C/G
Inside you there's a strength that lies, ____ lies.

Interlude 1

| E5 | | | | |

Verse 2

    E
Don't let your soul get lonely, child.

           Dmaj7
It's only time, it will go ____ by.

    E
Don't look for love in faces, places.

           Dmaj7   **C/G**
It's in you, that's where you'll ____ find kindness.

Chorus 1

```
E    C/G      Asus2         C/G
Be ___ here ___ now, here ___ now.

E    C/G      Asus2         C/G
Be ___ here ___ now, here ___ now.
```

Interlude 2   *Repeat Interlude 1*

Interlude 3

	E			
	Dmaj7			
	E			
|Dmaj7	|C/G		
	E5			

Verse 3

```
E
   Don't lose your faith in me

                            Dmaj7
And I will try not to lose faith in you.

E
   Don't put your trust in walls

                              Dmaj7      C/G
'Cause walls will only crush you when they ___ fall.
```

Chorus 2   *Repeat Chorus 1*

Interlude 4

	E			

Outro

	E			
	Dmaj7			
	E			
|Dmaj7	|C/G		
		|E5		
				|N.C.(E)

Burn

Words and Music by
Ray LaMontagne

Melody:

Oh, Ma - ma, don't walk ___ a - way.

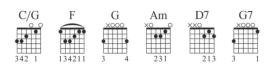

C/G   F   G   Am   D7   G7

342 1   134211   3   4   231   213   3   1

Intro

‖: C/G | | | :‖

Verse 1

    C/G   F
Oh, Mama, don't walk a - way.

      G   C/G
I'm a god - damn sore loser, I ain't too ___ proud to say.

           Am
But I'm still ___ thinking 'bout you,

           F
And I'm so ___ lonesome without you,

    D7   G G7
An' I can't get you out of my mind.

Verse 2

    C/G   F
Oh, Ma - ma, don't leave me a - lone

      G   C/G
With my soul shut down so tight just like a stone cold tomb.

       Am   F
Ain't it clear when I'm near you, I'm just ___ dying to hear you

D7   G G7
Callin' my name one more time.

Chorus

        F   Am   F   Am
Oh, so don't pay no mind ___ to my watering eyes.

        C/G   G
Must be something in the air that I'm breath - ing.

        F   Am   F   Am
Yes, and try to ignore   all this blood on the floor.

        C/G   G   G7
It's just this heart on my sleeve that's bleed - ing.

Verse 3

        C/G   F
Oh, Ma - ma, don't walk a - way.

        G   C/G
You leave me here bereavin' from the words ___ so hard and plain,

        Am   F
Sayin' the love that we had was just ___ selfish and sad.

        D7   F
Yes, but to see her now with him, it's just makin' me mad.

Outro

        C/G   G
Oh, so kiss him again just to prove ___ to me that you can.

        F   C/G
I will stand ___ here and burn in my skin.

        F   C/G
Yes, I will stand ___ here and burn in my skin.

Can I Stay

Words and Music by
Ray LaMontagne

Can I stay ___ here with you

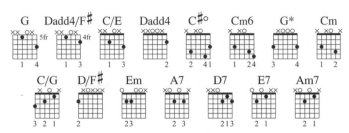

Intro

G Dadd4/F♯	C/E Dadd4	C♯° Cm6	G*
G Dadd4/F♯	C/E Dadd4	C♯° Cm	G* C/G
G*		C/G

Verse 1

G*   D/F♯   Em
Can I stay here with you till the morn - ing?

A7   D7
I am ___ so far from home and I feel ___ a little stoned.

G*   D/F♯   E7
Can I stay ___ here with you till the morn - ing?

Am7   D7
There's nothing I want more than to wake ___ up on your floor.

Chorus 1

Em   A7
Lay with me in your thinnest dress.

Em   A7
Fill my heart with each ___ caress.

D7
Between ___ your blissful kisses, whisper,

G*
"Darling, is this love?"

Interlude 1	|G Dadd4/F♯ |C/E Dadd4 |C♯° Cm6 |G* C/G |

          G*   D/F♯   Em

Verse 2   Can I stay here with you till the day ___ breaks?

            A7   D7

There's something you should know. I ain't got ___ no place to go.

              G*   D/F♯   E7

Can I stay ___ here with you till the day ___ breaks?

        Am7   D7

How happy it would make me to see ___ your face when I awake.

Chorus 2	*Repeat Chorus 1*
Interlude 2	*Repeat Interlude 1*

          G*   D/F♯   Em

Verse 3   Can I stay here with you through the night - time?

            A7   D7

I've fallen sad inside and I need ___ a place to hide.

              G*   D/F♯   E7

Can I stay ___ here with you through the night - time?

        Am7   D7

I'm all ___ alone and blue. Won't you take ___ me to your room?

Chorus 3	*Repeat Chorus 1*

          G   Dadd4/F♯ C/E Dadd4

Outro   Whis - per   to   me,

        C♯° Cm6 G*

        "Is   this   love?"

        |G   Dadd4/F♯ |C/E Dadd4 |C♯° Cm6 ||

Empty

Words and Music by
Ray LaMontagne

Melody:

She lifts her skirt up to her knees,

(Capo 2nd fret)

Am   F   C/G   E   C   G/B   G   E7

Intro

‖: Am | | | :‖

‖: F | | | |

| C/G | | | :‖

| Am | | | |

Verse 1

          F
She lifts her skirt up to her knees,

                                              C/G
Walks through the garden rows with her bare feet, laughin'.

                  F
I never learned ___ to count my blessings.

                       C/G
I choose instead to dwell in my disas - ters.

  Am   **E**
I walk on down the hill through grass grown tall and brown

            F   **C**   **G/B**
And still it's hard somehow to let go of my ___ pain.

Am   **E**
  On past the busted back of that old and rusted Cadillac

            F   **C**
That sinks ___ into this field collecting ___ rain.

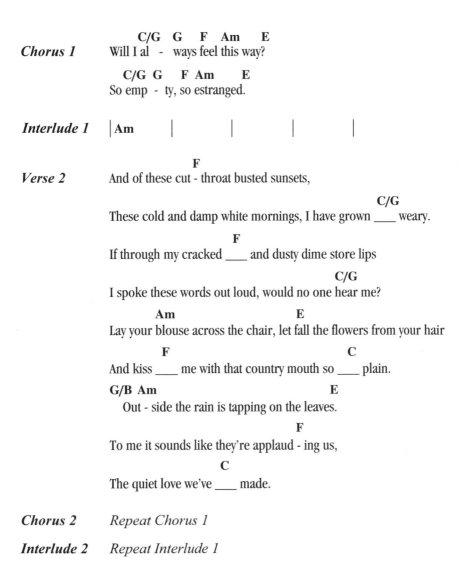

Chorus 1

        C/G   G   F Am   E
Will I al - ways feel this way?

        C/G G   F Am   E
So emp - ty, so estranged.

Interlude 1 | Am | | | |

Verse 2

                     F
And of these cut - throat busted sunsets,

                                               C/G
These cold and damp white mornings, I have grown ___ weary.

                       F
If through my cracked ___ and dusty dime store lips

                                     C/G
I spoke these words out loud, would no one hear me?

             Am   E
Lay your blouse across the chair, let fall the flowers from your hair

            F   C
And kiss ___ me with that country mouth so ___ plain.

G/B Am   E
   Out - side the rain is tapping on the leaves.

                                 F
To me it sounds like they're applaud - ing us,

                  C
The quiet love we've ___ made.

Chorus 2   *Repeat Chorus 1*

Interlude 2   *Repeat Interlude 1*

Instrumental ‖: F | | | |
         | C/G | | | :‖
         | Am | | | |

Verse 3

                     F
Well, I looked ___ my demons in the eyes,

                                   C/G
Laid bare my chest, said, "Do your best.   Destroy me."

                F
See, I've been ___ to hell and back so many times,

                         C/G
I must admit you kinda bore ___ me.

              Am   **E**
There's a lot of things that can kill a man, there's a lot of ways to die.

                     F   **C**
Yes, and some ___ already dead that walk beside ___ me.

G/B   **Am**
   There's a lot of things I don't understand,

              E
Why so ___ many people lie.

                 F   **C**
It's the hurt ___ I hide that fuels the fire in - side me.

Chorus 3

       C/G   **G**   **F**   **Am**   **E**
Will I al - ways feel this way?

       C/G   **G**   **F Am**   **E E7**
So emp - ty, so estranged.

Outro   ‖: Am | | | :‖   ‖

Hold You in My Arms

Words and Music by
Ray LaMontagne and Ethan Johns

When you came   to   me, _

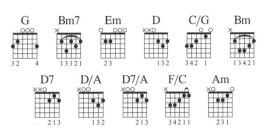

Intro

‖: G   Bm7 |Em   D |C/G | :‖

Verse 1

G   Bm
When you came to me,

Em   C/G
With your bad dreams and your fears,

       D7   G   D/A D7/A
Was easy to see you'd been crying.

G   Bm
Seems like ev'rywhere you turn,

Em   C/G
Catastrophe ____ reigns.

       D7   G   D/A D7/A
But who really profits from the dy - ing?

Chorus 1

Em   G   C/G F/C C/G
I could hold you in my arms.

D/A   D7/A   G D/A D7/A
I could hold you for - ever.

G   Bm   Em F/C C/G
And I could hold you in my arms, whoa, oo.

D/A   D7/A   G D/A D7/A
I could hold you for - ever.

Interlude 1   *Repeat Intro*

Verse 2

G   Bm
When you kissed my lips

Em   C/G
With my mouth so full of questions,

            D7   G D/A D7/A
My worried mind, that you qui - et.

G   Bm
Place your hands on my face,

Em   C/G
Close my eyes ____ and say

           D7
That love is a poor man's food.

G   D/A D7/A
Don't prophesize.

Chorus 2   *Repeat Chorus 1*

String Solo

Am		Bm		
Em		C/G		
	D/A D7/A			

Interlude 2   *Repeat Intro*

Verse 3

G   Bm
So, now we see how it is

Em   C/G
As fist begets ____ the spear.

                   D7   G   D/A D7/A
Weapons of war, ____ symptoms ____ of madness.

G   Bm
Don't let your eyes refuse to see.

Em   C/G
Don't let your ears ____ refuse to hear.

                   D7   G   D/A D7/A
You ain't nev - er gonna shake this sense ____ of sadness.

Chorus 3

Em   G   C/G   F/C C/G
I could hold you in my arms.

D/A   D7/A   G D/A D7/A
I could hold on for - ever.

G   Bm   Em F/C C/G
And I could hold you in my arms, whoa, oo.

D/A   D7/A   G D/A D7/A
I could hold on for - ever.

Outro

G Bm7	Em D	C/G		
		Ah.		
G Bm7	Em D	C/G		
					‖

For the Summer

Words and Music by
Ray LaMontagne

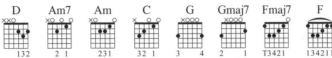

Tune down 1 step:
(low to high) D-G-C-F-A-D

D	Am7	Am	C	G	Gmaj7	Fmaj7	F
xxO	xO O O	xO O O	x O O	xOOO	xOOO		
132	2 1	231	32 1	3 4	2 1	T3421	134211

Intro |D |Am7 |D |Am7 |

Verse 1
```
      D      Am        C
  Rollin' through these hills

      G        D          Am C G
I've known I'd ___ be comin'.

  D         Am      C
  Ain't a man ___ alive

              G            D Am C G
That likes ___ to be alone.
```

Verse 2
```
      D         Am
  Been a while

        C          G        D Am C G
Since I ___ seen my la - dy smile.

  D          Am
  Have I been,

        C       G        D Am C G
Have I been away ___ so long?
```

Pre-Chorus 1

      C   G
I am tired.

      C   G
I am tired.

Chorus 1

D   Am7
Can I come home ___ for the summer?

Gmaj7   Fmaj7   D
I could slow down for a little while.

          Am7
Get back to lov - in' each other,

Gmaj7   Fmaj7
Leave all those long and lonesome miles behind.

Interlude

‖: D   Am |C   G   :‖

Verse 3

D   Am
Through the years

     C   G   D   Am C G
I have learned some ___ things worth the tellin'.

D   Am
And you'd be right ___ in guessin'

C   G   D   Am C G
That each and ev'ry les - son they were hard won.

Pre-Chorus 2   *Repeat Pre-Chorus 1*

Chorus 2   *Repeat Chorus 1*

Guitar Solo

‖: D   Am |C   G   :‖ *Play 4 times*

Outro

D   Am7   D   Am7
You'll follow her   wher - ever she goes.

D   Am7   G   F   D
You love her and you just want ___ her to know

         Am7   D   Am7
That you'll follow her,   you'll find a way.

D   Am7   G   F   D
You love her and you just want ___ her to know.

Gossip in the Grain

Words and Music by
Ray LaMontagne

Melody:

Such the la - zy Jack - straw, ___

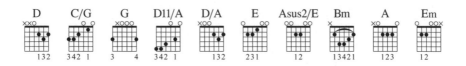

D   C/G   G   D11/A   D/A   E   Asus2/E   Bm   A   Em

Intro

| $\frac{4}{4}$ D | | $\frac{2}{4}$ | $\frac{4}{4}$ C/G | G | |
| $\frac{3}{4}$ D   G D11/A | $\frac{4}{4}$ C/G | | |

Verse 1

D   C/G   G
Such the lazy Jackstraw, ____ always late for tea,

               D/A G   D11/A C/G
Never bothers to   ring late - ly.

D/A   C/G   G
Says the silly Sparrow, ____ "Gossip in the grain.

               D/A G   D11/A C/G
Have you heard the… Oh, you don't   say."

Chorus 1

C/G   G   D11/A
"Someday, ____ someday,

            C/G
A snow shall fill ____ the trees.

D11/A   E
  You'd best make warm ____ the eaves."

| *Interlude 1* | │C/G   │Asus2/E │C/G   │   │ |

Verse 2

D/A   C/G   G
Callous is the old crow, ___ he'd mock even the sun.

                  D/A   G   D11/A C/G
Eyes as black as blood, bone crack in ___ the craw.

Chorus 2

C/G   G   D11/A
He'd say, ___ he'd say

             C/G
Always a "Never mind,"

D11/A   E
  Always a "Never mind."

Interlude 2

│C/G   │Asus2/E │D11/A │E   │
│C/G   │Asus2/E │C/G   │   │

Outro

D/A   G   Bm
Truth be: Beggar that holds his tongue

A   Em   D/A   A   G
Dines on ___ none, none but air a - lone.

How Come

Words and Music by
Ray LaMontagne

Melody:

Peo - ple on the street, __ now, __

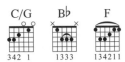

```
C/G        Bb         F
342 1      1333       134211
```

Intro   ‖: C/G Bb F | Bb C/G | Bb F | Bb C/G :‖

Verse 1

C/G   Bb
   People on the street, now,

F   Bb
   Faces long and grim.

C/G   Bb
   Souls are feelin' heavy and

F   Bb   F
   Faith is growing ___ thin.

C/G   Bb
   Fears are gettin' stronger,

F   Bb
You feel them on the rise.

C/G   Bb
   Hopelessness got some by the throat.

   F
You can see it in their eyes.

Chorus 1

Bb   C/G   Bb F
I said, how come?

Bb C/G   Bb F   Bb C/G
  How come?

Verse 2

C/G   Bb
  Ev'rybody on a shoestring,

F   Bb
  Ev'rybody in a hole,

C/G   Bb
  Ev'rybody on his own jet plane

F   Bb F
  Crossin' their fingers and toes.

C/G   Bb F
  Government man spin his politics

           Bb
Till they've got you pinned.

C/G   Bb
  Ev'rybody tryin' to reach out to each oth - er,

  F
But they don't know where to begin.

Chorus 2

    C/G   Bb
I said, how come I can't tell

F
The free world from a living hell?

Bb C/G   Bb F
I said, how come?

Bb C/G   Bb F
   How come all I see ___ is a child of God in misery,

Bb C/G   Bb F   Bb C/G
I said, how come?

Guitar Solo 1 | C/G   B♭ F | B♭   C/G | B♭   F | B♭ C/G |

Verse 3

C/G   B♭
   The pistol now as prophet,

F   B♭
   The bullet some kinda lord and king,

C/G
But pain is the only promise

B♭   F   B♭   F
   That this so-called savior's gon - na bring.

C/G   B♭
   Love can be a liar,

F   B♭
   And justice can be a thief.

C/G
And freedom can be an empty cup

B♭   F
From which ev'rybody wanna drink.

Chorus 3

B♭ F   C/G   B♭
   I said, how come I can't tell

F
The free world from a living hell?

B♭   C/G   B♭   F
I said,   how come?

B♭   C/G   B♭   F
   How come all I see ___ is a child of God in misery,

B♭   C/G   B♭   F
I said,   how come?

Bridge

Bb   C/G   Bb F
It's just man killin' man, killin' man, ___ killin' man, killin' man.

 Bb C/G   Bb F
I don't understand.

Bb   C/G   Bb F
It's just man killin' man, killin' man, ___ killin' man, killin' man.

 Bb C/G   Bb F
I don't understand it.

Bb   C/G   Bb
It's just man killin' man, killin' man,

F   Bb C/G
Killin' man, killin' man, kill - in' man,

                 Bb   F
Killin' man, killin' man,   kill - in' man, killin' man.

 Bb C/G   Bb   F
I don't   understand it. I don't   understand it.

Bb C/G   Bb   F   Bb
I don't   understand it. I don't   understand it.

C/G   Bb F   Bb
How come? I said,   how come?

C/G   Bb F   Bb C/G
How come? I said,   how come?

**Outro-
Guitar Solo**   *Repeat Guitar Solo 1 and fade*

I Still Care for You

Words and Music by
Ray LaMontagne

Melody:

Hear ____ me ____ out. _____

Tune down 1 step:
(low to high) D-G-C-F-A-D

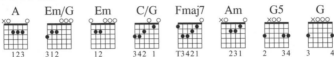

A   Em/G   Em   C/G   Fmaj7   Am   G5   G

123   312   12   342 1   T3421   231   2 34   3   4

Intro   ‖: A |Em/G | | | :‖

Verse 1
A   Em
Hear ____ me out.

C/G   Fmaj7
Day fol - lows day.

Am   C/G   Fmaj7
Light turns ____ to clay in my hands.

A   Em
How to explain,

C/G   Fmaj7   Am
So pris - tine the pain.

                    C/G   Fmaj7
Kindness made ____ the cut so ____ clean.

Chorus 1
Am   C/G   Fmaj7   G5
I still ____ care ____ for you.

Am   C/G   Fmaj7   G5
I still ____ care ____ for you.

Am   C/G   Fmaj7
I still ____ care ____ for you.

| *Interlude 1* | |A |Em/G | | | | |

Verse 2

A   Em
Hear ___ me out.

C/G   Fmaj7
Wanted me ___ to be

Am   C/G   Fmaj7
Less your lov - er than a mirror.

A   Em
Can't ___ you see

C/G   Fmaj7
What you mean ___ to me?

Am   C/G   Fmaj7
Even prom - ises may bleed.

Chorus 2   *Repeat Chorus 1*

Interlude 2   *Repeat Interlude 1*

Bridge

    C/G G
The hours grow

C/G   Fmaj7 Am G
Heavy and hol   -   low.

C/G   Fmaj7
Cruel as a grave.

C/G G C/G   Fmaj7
O - pen me and you'll find

Am G C/G   Fmaj7   A Em/G
On - ly bones burned ___ to glass.

Chorus 3   *Repeat Chorus 1*

Outro |A |Em/G | |A |
          |Em/G | | | |
          |A ||

Jolene

Words and Music by
Ray LaMontagne

Melody:

Co - caine flame in my blood - stream, ___

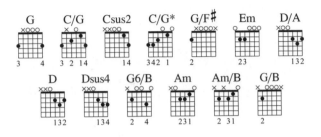

G   C/G   Csus2   C/G*   G/F#   Em   D/A

D   Dsus4   G6/B   Am   Am/B   G/B

Intro
‖: G   C/G   Csus2 │C/G   G   C/G :‖

Verse 1

    G   C/G*   G
Cocaine flame in my bloodstream,

                C/G*
Sold my coat when I hit ___ Spokane.

Bought myself a hard pack of cigarettes

                G C/G
In the early mornin' rain.

G
   Lately my hands, they don't feel like mine.

          C/G*
My eyes been stung with dust, I'm blind.

Held you in my arms one time.

           G G/F#
Lost you just the same.

Chorus 1

Em   G C/G*   G
  Jolene, ____ I ain't a - bout

D/A Em   G   C/G*
To go   straight. ____ It's too late.

         G   C/G   G
I found ___ myself face down in the ditch,

         D   Dsus4   D
Booze ___ in my hair, blood on my lips,

  C/G*
A picture of you holdin' a picture of me

               G G/F♯
In the pocket of my blue jeans.

Em   G   C/G*
  Still don't know what love ___ means.

Em   G   C/G*   G6/B Am Am/B
  Still don't know what love ___ means.

C G6/B Am   G
             Jolene,

        C/G*   G/B   Am
La, la, la, ____ la, la, ____ la, la.

  Jolene.

Interlude

|G C/G Csus2 |C/G G C/G |G C/G Csus2 |C/G G C/G |

Verse 2

G
  Been so long since I've seen your face

         C/G*
Or felt a part of this human race.

I've been livin' outta this here suitcase

         G C/G
For way too long.

G
  A man needs somethin' he can hold on to.

         C/G*
Nine pound hammer or a woman like you.

           G G/F♯
Either one of them things will do.

Chorus 2

      Em   G C/G*   G
      Jolene, ____   I ain't a - bout

D/A Em   G   C/G*
To go   straight. ____ It's too late.

           G   C/G   G
I found ___ myself face down in the ditch,

         D   Dsus4   D
Booze ___ in my hair, blood on my lips,

  C/G*
A picture of you holdin' a picture of me

                       G G/F♯
In the pocket of my blue jeans.

Em   G   C/G*
   Still don't know what love ___ means.

Em   G   C/G*   G6/B Am Am/B
   Still don't know what love ___ means.

C G6/B Am   G
                Jolene,

         C/G*   G/B   Am
La, la, la, ___ la, la, ___ la, la.

          G   C/G*   G/B   Am
Jolene, ___ la, la, la, ___ la, la, ___ la, la.

Jolene.

Outro | G C/G Csus2 | C/G G C/G | G C/G Csus2 | C/G G ‖

Shelter

Words and Music by
Ray LaMontagne

I guess you   don't   need _ it,

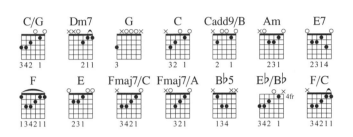

Intro   ‖: C/G Dm7 | G C Cadd9/B | Am E7 | F   C/G G :‖

Verse 1

    C/G   Dm7
    I guess you   don't need it.

G   C   C/B   Am
    I guess you don't   want me to repeat it,

                 E7   F   C/G G
But ev'rything I have to give, I'll give to you.

C/G   Dm7
    It's not like ____ we planned it.

G   C   C/B   Am
    You tried to stay ____ but you could not stand it

                  E   F   C/G
To see me shut down ____ slow as though it was an easy thing to do.

Chorus 1

```
         G          C/G                 Fmaj7/C
Listen, when    all of this around ___ us will fall over,
```

```
                                   C/G
I tell you what we're gonna do, ___ hey.
```

```
           E            F          C/G  G
You will   shelter me, ___ my love,
```

```
C/G    Dm7      G           Fmaj7/A
And I, ___ I will shelter you, ___ oh.
```

```
           C/G         Dm7 G   C  Cadd9/B
I will shel - ter you.
```

```
| Am  E7   |F   C/G  G |
```

Verse 2

```
C/G    Dm7
 I left ___ you heartbroken,
```

```
G                      C            C/B
 But not until those ___ very words ___ were spoken.
```

```
Am           E7                F          C/G  G
 Has anybody ever made such a fool outta you?
```

```
C/G          Dm7
 It's hard to ___ believe it,
```

```
G            C   C/B    Am
 Even as my eyes ___ do see it.
```

```
                   E                 F        C/G
The very things that, uh, make you live are killin' you.
```

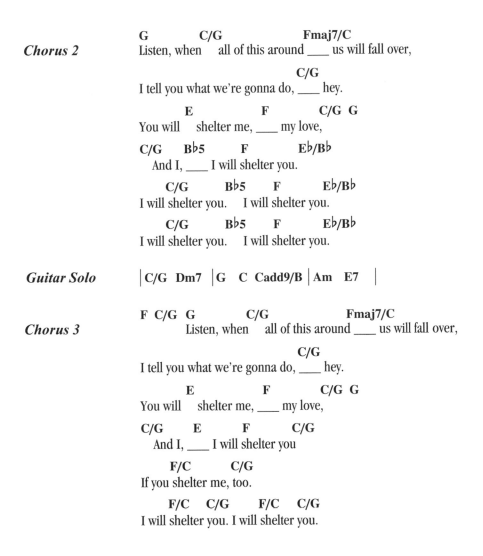

Chorus 2

G   C/G   Fmaj7/C
Listen, when   all of this around ___ us will fall over,

                        C/G
I tell you what we're gonna do, ___ hey.

          E   F   C/G G
You will   shelter me, ___ my love,

C/G   Bb5   F   Eb/Bb
And I, ___ I will shelter you.

      C/G   Bb5   F   Eb/Bb
I will shelter you.   I will shelter you.

      C/G   Bb5   F   Eb/Bb
I will shelter you.   I will shelter you.

Guitar Solo

|C/G Dm7 |G   C Cadd9/B |Am   E7 |

Chorus 3

F C/G G   C/G   Fmaj7/C
          Listen, when   all of this around ___ us will fall over,

                        C/G
I tell you what we're gonna do, ___ hey.

          E   F   C/G G
You will   shelter me, ___ my love,

C/G   E   F   C/G
And I, ___ I will shelter you

      F/C   C/G
If you shelter me, too.

      F/C   C/G   F/C   C/G
I will shelter you. I will shelter you.

Lavender

Words and Music by
Ray LaMontagne

Tune down 1/2 step:
(low to high) E♭-A♭-D♭-G♭-B♭-E♭

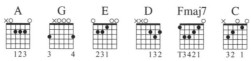

Intro

A G	E D		**2/4**	
4/4 A				

Verse 1

A   G E
We lie under a lavender sky.

Fmaj7   A
 Under a lavender sky ___ we lie.

             G E
Do you, do you remember the day?

Fmaj7   A
 Do you remember when we felt that way?

        E   D
Free to play, ___ as a child ___ we ran

         C
Through fields ___ of clover

     A   E   D C A
Un - derneath the ___ sun.

Verse 2

    A   G E
Back there, both of us without a care.

Fmaj7   A
Leaves of many colors blown through the air.

                   E   D
Free to play, ____ as a child ____ we ran

                  C
Through fields ____ of clover

        A   E
Reach - ing for the ____ sun. (Reaching for the sun.)

Bridge

Fmaj7   **D**   **Fmaj7**   **D**
I'll count twenty-five.   No fair, cover your eyes!

A   C   **Fmaj7**   A
Go on run and hide.   You'll never find me!

C   **Fmaj7** A
Find me! Find me! Find me!

Guitar Solo

‖: A | | | :‖
| | |

Verse 3

    A   G E
We lie under a lavender sky.

Fmaj7   A
Under a lavender sky ____ we lie.

                   E   D
Free to play, ____ running cir - cles

                  C
'Round the place ____ we found

        A   E
That no ____ one ever ____ knew. (No one ever knew.)

Outro   *Repeat Bridge*

Let It Be Me

Words and Music by
Ray LaMontagne

Melody:

There comes __ a time, __

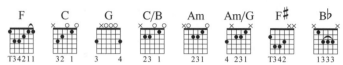

F C G C/B Am Am/G F♯ B♭

Intro

N.C.	F			
	C			
	G			
	F		C	

Verse 1

F   C
There comes a time,   a time in ev'ryone's life
G
When nothing seems to go your way,
F   C
When nothing seems to turn out right.
F   G
There may ___ come a time,
C   C/B   Am   Am/G
You just can't seem to find your place.
F   G   N.C. F♯
And for ev'ry door you open,
F   G
Seems like you get two slammed in your face.

Pre-Chorus 1

            N.C.   F   B♭   F
That's   when you need someone,
                C   F   C
Someone that you, you can call
            G
When all your faith is gone,
              F   C
It feels like you can't go on.

Copyright © 2008 BMG Monarch and Sweet Mary Music
All Rights Administered by BMG Rights Management (US) LLC
All Rights Reserved   Used by Permission

40

GUITAR CHORD SONGBOOK

Chorus 1	**F** **C** Let it be ___ me, let it be me.

    G
If it's a friend that you need,

     F   **C**
Let it be ___ me, let it be me.

Verse 2

F
  Feels like you're always comin' up last.

C
  Pockets full of nothing, ain't got no cash.

G
  No matter where you turn, you ain't got no place to stand, yeah.

F   **C**
  You reach out for somethin' and they slap your hand.

F   **G**
  I remember all too well,

C   **C/B**   **Am** **Am/G**
  Just how ___ it feels to be all alone,

F   **G**   **N.C.** **F♯**
  To feel like you'd give anything

F   **G**
  For just a little place you can call ___ your own.

Pre-Chorus 2	*Repeat Pre-Chorus 1*
Chorus 2	*Repeat Chorus 1*

Outro-Chorus

     F   **C**
Let it be ___ me, let it be me.

    G   **F**
If it's a friend you need, let it be me,

    G   **C**
Let it be ___ me, let it be ___ me.

Supernova

Words and Music by
Ray LaMontagne

Zo - e, you and me, we've been hang - in' out __ now, __

Tune down 1/2 step:
(low to high) Eb-Ab-Db-Gb-Bb-Eb

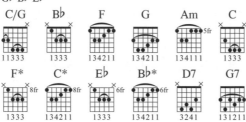

Intro |C/G | | |

Verse 1
> C/G   Bb   F
> Zoe, you and me, we've been hangin' out now
>
>   Bb   G
> Ever since we were kids, just kicking a - round this town.
>
> C/G   Bb   F
> Zoe, you know me and I don't back down
>
>   Bb   G
> When I know what I want, and I think I found it.

Pre-Chorus 1
> F   Am   G
> I want you ___ to be my girl.
>
> F   Am   G
> I want you ___ to be my girl.

Chorus 1

C   F   C   G
Zoe, just a Superno - va!

C   F   C   G
Zoe, just a Superno - va! *Super!*

Verse 2

C/G   B♭   F
  Zoe, you know me and I'm on the right track.

                          B♭   G
Gonna get outta here an' never come back. *Uh-uh!*

C/G   B♭   F
  Zoe, you know me when I'm on the attack,

               B♭   G
Ain't no use in fighting back.

Pre-Chorus 2   *Repeat Pre-Chorus 1*

Chorus 2   *Repeat Chorus 1*

Interlude   ‖: F* C* E♭ | B♭* C | G | :‖
                                        (Supernova.)

	F G
Bridge	When I'm low, well, I know who to call.

C   Am
When I think I'm 'bout to hit the wall,

F   D7
Zoe, baby, I know that you ___ would never,

          G   G7
Never let ___ me fall.

F   G
Ev'rytime I turn around, baby, there you are,

C   Am
Just shinin' down on me like a blaz - ing star.

F   D7   G
Yeah, that's what you are, you're a blaz - ing star,

                          G7
That's what you are. That's what you are. That's what, what, what, what.

Chorus 3   *Repeat Chorus 1*

Verse 3   *Repeat Verse 1*

Pre-Chorus 3   *Repeat Pre-Chorus 1*

	C F C G
Chorus 4	‖: Zoe, just a Superno - va!

C   F   C   G
Zoe, just a Superno - va! :‖ *Super!*

Outro	‖: F* C* Eb │ Bb* C │G │ :‖
	(Supernova.)

│ F* C* Eb │ Bb* C │G

Three More Days

Melody:

Three _ more days. _   Girl, you know I   will _

Words and Music by
Ray LaMontagne

Tune down 1 step:
(low to high) D-G-C-F-A-D

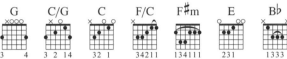

| G | C/G | C | F/C | F♯m | E | B♭ |

Intro
‖: G   C/G | G   C/G :‖

Verse 1

G   C/G
  Three more days.

G   C/G   G
  Girl, you know I will ____ be com - in' home

               C/G G C/G
To you, darlin'.

C   F/C
  Three more days.

C   G
  Girl, you know I will be com - in' home

               C/G G F♯m
To you, darlin'.

Pre-Chorus 1

E   G   F♯m E
  I know it's wrong to be so far from home.

                          G   F♯m E
I know it's wrong to leave you so alone.

                        C
I've just got to get-cha this good job done

N.C.
So I can bring it on…

Chorus 1

G
Home to you,

C   G   C
So I can bring it on home to you.

Interlude 1   ‖: G   C/G | G   C/G :‖

Verse 2

G   C/G
Three more days.

G   C/G   G
Girl, you know I will ___ be right ___ there

                  C/G G C/G
By your side, ba - by.

C   F/C
Three more days.

C   G
Girl, you know I will be right ___ there

                  C/G G F#m
By your side, ba - by.

Pre-Chorus 2

E   G   F#m E
I know it's wrong to leave you ___ so alone.

                      G   F#m E
I know it's wrong to be so far from home.

                        C
I've just got to get-cha this good job done

N.C.
So I can bring it on…

Chorus 2

       G
Home to ya,

    C   G   C
  So I can bring it on home to ya.

Interlude 2 | G | Bb | C | G |

Bridge

                 G   Bb   C
Gonna bring it on home to ya, home to ya, home to ya.

       G
I said listen, uh, uh, listen, uh. I'll bring it on, uh,

        Bb   C
Home to ya, home to ya, ah. Bring it on home to ya.

       G
I said listen, uh, uh, listen, uh, uh, listen, uh.

                          Bb
Gonna get it so ya can't say no.   Gonna give it so ya can't say no.

C
  Gonna give it so ya can't say no.

G
Give it to ya, give it to ya, give it to ya.

                          Bb
Gonna give it so ya can't say no.   Gonna give it so ya can't say no.

C   G
  Gonna give it so ya can't say no.

Outro ||: G | C | G | C   :|| *Repeat and fade*

Trouble

Words and Music by
Ray LaMontagne

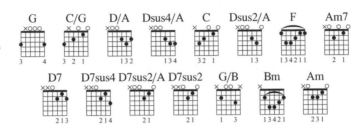

Trou-ble, _____   trou-ble, trou - ble,

Intro

‖: G C/G │ G D/A Dsus4/A D/A :‖ *Play 4 times*

Verse 1

G   D/A G   C/G
Trouble, ___ trouble, trouble, ___ trouble, trouble.

G   D/A
Trouble been doggin' my soul

            C   G D/A Dsus2/A D/A
Since the day I was born, ah.

G   D/A G   C/G
Worry, ___ worry, worry, worry, worry.

G   D/A   C
Worry just will not seem to leave my mind alone.

Chorus 1

G D/A   N.C.   G   C
Well, I've been, uh, saved by ___ a woman.

F C   G   C
I've been, uh, saved by ___ a woman.

F C   G   C
I've been, uh, saved by ___ a woman.

F C   Am7   D7
She won't let me go, she won't let me go, now.

D7sus4 D7 D7sus2/A Am7
She won't let me go

          D7   D7sus2
She won't let me go now, now.

Interlude 1 ‖: G   C/G |G   D/A   Dsus4/A   D/A   :‖

Verse 2

G   D/A   G   C/G
Trouble, ___ oh, ___ trouble, trou - ble, trouble, trouble.

G   D/A
Feels like ev'ry time I get back on my feet,

                        C   G   D/A Dsus2/A D/A
She come around ___ and knock me down a - gain.

G   D/A   G   C/G
Worry, ___ oh, ___ wor - ry, worry, worry, worry.

G   D/A   C
Sometimes I swear it feels like this worry ___ is my only friend.

Chorus 2

G D/A   N.C.   G   C
    Well, I've been, uh, saved by ___ a woman.

F C   G   C
    I've been, uh, saved by ___ a woman.

F C   G   C
    I've been, uh, saved by ___ a woman.

G/B   Am7   D7
    She won't let me go, she won't let me go, now.

D7sus4 D7 D7sus2/A   Am7
                She won't let me go,

            D7
She won't let me go now, now.

RAY LAMONTAGNE   **49**

Bridge

    C   Bm Am G
    Oh, ____   ah,

    C   Bm
    Oh.

    Am   G   C/G G
    Mm, she good ____ to me, now.

    C/G   G C/G   G
    She give me love ____ and af - fection.

    C/G   G   C/G G
    Say she good ____ to me, now.

    C/G   G C/G   G
    She give me love ____ and af - fection.

    C/G   G   C/G   G
    I said, I love her.   Yes, I love her.

    C/G   G   C/G   G C/G
    I said, I love her.   I said, I love.

      G   C/G G
    She good ____ to me, now.

    C/G G   C/G   G   C/G
    She good to me.   She good to me.

Outro

    G C/G G C/G   G
    Mm, _____ mm,

    C/G G C/G G C/G G
    Mm, ____ mm.

You Are the Best Thing

Words and Music by
Ray LaMontagne

Ba - by, __   it's been a long day.

Tune down 1 step:
(low to high) D-G-C-F-A-D

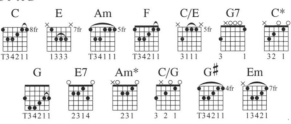

Intro   N.C. | C E Am | F | C E Am | F |
            | C E Am | C/E F | G7 C* | G7 |

Verse 1
         C*   G Am
         Baby,

                 F   C*
         It's been a long day.

              G Am
         Baby,

                          F
         Things ain't been going my way.

                    C*   G   Am
         You know I ___ need you ___ here.

              F   G7
         You clear my mind ___ all the time.

         C*   G Am
           And, baby,

                      F   C*   G Am
         The way you move me, it's cra - zy.

                    F   C*   G Am
         It's like you see right through me and make it easier.

              F   G7
         You please me, you don't even   have to try.

Chorus 1

          C*   E7   Am*   F
Oh, because ___ you are the best thing. (You're the best thing.)

C*   E7   Am*   F
 You are the best thing. (You're the best thing, baby.)

C*   E7   Am   C/G   F
 You are the best thing (You're the best thing, oo.)

   G7   C*   G
Ever happened to me.

Verse 2

C*   G Am
 Baby,

            F
We've come a ___ long way.

C*   G Am
 Baby,

          F   **C***   **G Am**
You know I hope and I pray that you'll believe me

           F   **G7**
When I say ___ this love will ___ never fade away.

Chorus 2

          C*   E7   Am*   F
Oh, because ___ you are the best thing. (You're the best thing.)

C*   E7   Am*   F
 You are the best thing. (You're the best thing, baby.)

C*   E7   Am*   C/G   F
 You are the best thing (You're the best thing, oo.)

   G7   C*   G G♯
Ever happened to me.

Bridge

```
Am                      Em
   Both of us have known love before

Am                           Em
   To come on all promising like the spring,

   E7            F
To walk on out the door.

                            C*
Our hearts are strong and our,    our hearts are kind.

F                      G7
   Let me tell you just ex - actly what's on my mind.
```

Chorus 3

```
   C*    E7    Am*                F
‖:   You are the best thing. (You're the best thing.)

C*    E7    Am*                 F
   You are the best thing. (You're the best thing, baby.)

C*    E7    Am*              C/G      F
   You are the best thing (You're the best thing, oo.)

   G7          C*    G
Ever happened to me.        :‖
```

Outro-Chorus

```
C*    E7    Am*              F
   (You are the best thing.) Yeah, ___ yeah, yeah.

C*    E7    Am*    F
   (You are the best thing.) Yeah, yeah, yeah.

C*    E7    Am*    C/G  F
   (You are the best thing

        G7          C*
That ever happened to me.)
```

You Can Bring Me Flowers

Words and Music by
Ray LaMontagne

Her eyes _ have dried, _____ my

(Capo 3rd fret)

E5   A5

Intro   ‖: E5 |A5 |E5 |A5   :‖ *Play 4 times*

Verse 1
E5   A5   E5   A5
   Her eyes have dried, my   hands are tied.

E5 A5   E5 A5
   Nothin' I can say.

E5   A5   E5   A5
   If you feel the need ___ to go,

E5   A5   E5 A5
   I won't stand ___ in your way.

Chorus 1
A5
   Sit and think, and drown in drink.

Sing this sad, sad song.

E5   A5   E5   A5
   You can bring ___ me flowers, baby,

E5   A5   E5 A5
   When I'm ___ dead and gone.

Interlude 1 | E5 |A5 |E5 |A5 |

                 | E5 |A5 |E5 N.C. | |

                 ‖: E5 |A5 |E5 |A5   :‖

Verse 2

E5   A5   E5   A5
Fate has ____ played his hand so cruel.

E5   A5   E5 A5
There ain't nothin' I can do.

E5   A5   E5   A5
You say you lost your love ____ for me,

E5   A5   E5 A5
Me, my love ____ for you.

Chorus 2

A5
Sit and cry, and say goodbye,

And sing this sad, sad song.

E5   A5   E5   A5
You can ____ bring me flowers, baby,

E5   A5   E5 A5
When I'm ____ dead and gone.

Interlude 2

‖: E5 | A5 | E5 N.C. | :‖
‖: E5 | A5 | E5 | A5 :‖

Verse 3

E5   A5 E5 A5
So when you're ____ lyin' in his arms,

E5   A5   E5 A5
Think of ____ me and know

E5   A5 E5   A5
The choice you made ain't free and clear,

E5   A5   E5 A5
It cost me a ____ heavy toll.

Chorus 3   *Repeat Chorus 1*

Interlude 3

‖: E5 | A5 | E5 N.C. | :‖
| E5 | A5 | E5 | A5 |
| E5 | A5 | E5 N.C. | |
‖: E5 | A5 | E5 | A5 |
| E5 | A5 | E5 | A5 :‖

Outro-Flute Solo ‖: E5 | A5 | E5 | A5 :‖ *Repeat and fade*

RAY LAMONTAGNE

Guitar Chord Songbooks

Each book includes complete lyrics, chord symbols, and guitar chord diagrams.

Acoustic Hits
00701787 . . . . $14.99

Acoustic Rock
00699540 . . . . $17.95

Alabama
00699914 . . . . $14.95

The Beach Boys
00699566 . . . . $14.95

The Beatles (A-I)
00699558 . . . . $17.99

The Beatles (J-Y)
00699562 . . . . $17.99

Bluegrass
00702585 . . . . $14.99

Blues
00699733 . . . . $12.95

Broadway
00699920 . . . . $14.99

Johnny Cash
00699648 . . . . $17.99

Steven Curtis Chapman
00700702 . . . . $17.99

Children's Songs
00699539 . . . . $16.99

Christmas Carols
00699536 . . . . $12.99

Christmas Songs
00699537 . . . . $12.95

Eric Clapton
00699567 . . . . $15.99

Classic Rock
00699598 . . . . $15.99

Coffeehouse Hits
00703318 . . . . $14.99

Country
00699534 . . . . $14.95

Country Favorites
00700609 . . . . $14.99

Country Standards
00700608 . . . . $12.95

Cowboy Songs
00699636 . . . . $12.95

Creedence Clearwater Revival
00701786 . . . . $12.99

Crosby, Stills & Nash
00701609 . . . . $12.99

John Denver
02501697 . . . . $14.99

Neil Diamond
00700606 . . . . $14.99

Disney
00701071 . . . . $14.99

The Doors
00699888 . . . . $15.99

Best of Bob Dylan
14037617 . . . . $17.99

Early Rock
00699916 . . . . $14.99

Folk Pop Rock
00699651 . . . . $14.95

Folksongs
00699541 . . . . $12.95

40 Easy Strumming Songs
00115972 . . . . $14.99

Four Chord Songs
00701611 . . . . $12.99

Glee
00702501 . . . . $14.99

Gospel Hymns
00700463 . . . . $14.99

Grand Ole Opry®
00699885 . . . . $16.95

Green Day
00103074 . . . . $12.99

Guitar Chord Songbook White Pages
00702609 . . . . $29.99

Hillsong United
00700222 . . . . $12.95

Irish Songs
00701044 . . . . $14.99

Billy Joel
00699632 . . . . $15.99

Elton John
00699732 . . . . $15.99

Latin Songs
00700973 . . . . $14.99

Love Songs
00701043 . . . . $14.99

Bob Marley
00701704 . . . . $12.99

Paul McCartney
00385035 . . . . $16.95

Steve Miller
00701146 . . . . $12.99

Modern Worship
00701801 . . . . $16.99

Motown
00699734 . . . . $16.95

The 1950s
00699922 . . . . $14.99

The 1980s
00700551 . . . . $16.99

Nirvana
00699762 . . . . $16.99

Rock Ballads
00701034 . . . . $14.99

Roy Orbison
00699752 . . . . $12.95

Peter, Paul & Mary
00103013 . . . . $12.99

Tom Petty
00699883 . . . . $15.99

Pop/Rock
00699538 . . . . $14.95

Praise & Worship
00699634 . . . . $14.99

Elvis Presley
00699633 . . . . $14.95

Queen
00702395 . . . . $12.99

Red Hot Chili Peppers
00699710 . . . . $16.95

Rock Ballads
00701034 . . . . $14.99

Rock 'n' Roll
00699535 . . . . $14.95

Bob Seger
00701147 . . . . $12.99

Sting
00699921 . . . . $14.99

Taylor Swift
00701799 . . . . $15.99

Three Chord Songs
00699720 . . . . $12.95

Top 100 Hymns
75718017 . . . . $12.99

Two-Chord Songs
00119236 . . . . $14.99

Ultimate
00702617 . . . . $24.99

Wedding Songs
00701005 . . . . $14.99

Hank Williams
00700607 . . . . $14.99

Neil Young – Decade
00700464 . . . . $14.99

Prices, contents, and availability subject to change without notice.